POSITIVE
CLASSROOM PERFORMANCE
Techniques
for Changing Behavior

Patricia A. Gallagher
University of Kansas

Love Publishing Company Denver, Colorado 80222

EDUCATION SERIES

dedicated to all school age children
especially my Soesterberg class

Table of Contents

Introduction

Teachers are on the front line of action. They are engaged in daily contact with a myriad of classroom behaviors and are directly responsible for positive academic and social growth in school age children. Growth occurs when instructional techniques, motivation procedures, interpersonal relationships, meaningful curriculum materials, and an active learning environment are provided. The majority of students respond appropriately under these conditions, but there are instances when students do not participate in the learning tasks. Sometimes these situations get out of hand and the students' behavior becomes increasingly difficult to change. A variety of resources can be used to modify the teacher's approach in reaching the student with problems. This book will focus on helping such students by discussing and illustrating ideas for positive changes through the planned and consistent use of consequences.

A consequence is the event which follows an individual's

action and determines the probability of its future occurrence. Teachers apply consequences to behavior frequently, but sometimes these do not bring about the anticipated change. When a student does not complete an assignment, a negative type of consequence may follow, e.g., the student must relinquish recess and remain in the classroom to finish the assignment. If the student continues to produce incomplete assignments despite a growing number of missed recess periods, then it is reasonable to assume that missing recess is not an effective consequence. In fact, missing recess may not even be a consequence at all. When a student receives 100% on his paper, a positive consequence such as, display of the paper on the bulletin board may follow. If the student is sporadic in achieving high percentage grades then the bulletin board display of good papers is not an effective consequence for him. Teachers must constantly be aware of the consequences they use and try to vary their procedure so that these will be effective for and benefit the individual student.

It is important to note that individual consequences can be as effectively employed by the regular classroom teacher who has three or four children in need of special help as by the special class teacher who has a small class of children with chronic academic and behavior problems. In both cases a certain amount of teacher time and thought is involved in the selection and consistent application of consequences but the hours spent will pay great dividends in terms of the child's progress.

A PROGRAM FOR POSITIVE CHANGE

For consequences to be effective in changing classroom behavior several steps must be carefully implemented: (1) the selection of a target behavior, (2) finding a consequence which will "work," (3) discussion and clarification with the student of the arangement between the behavior and its consequence, (4) a plan for evaluation, and (5) fading the consequence. An explanation of these steps will provide the framework in which the examples, following this introduction, worked successfully in classrooms.

1. Select a target behavior. In order to bring about change it is important to pinpoint a specific behavior, i.e., one which is overt and observable such as, "reading-new-words behavior," "raising-hand behavior," or "insulting-gestures behavior." Frequently the student requiring special attention is the student who has exhibited many inappropriate behaviors which might include "messy papers," "inaccurate math calculations," "poor reading comprehension," "refusal to do homework," and "fighting in the halls." Jot down these behaviors and select *one* for modification. To insure a measure of success for the student, do not complicate the plan by embarking on a total "reform" program. Guide the student to change one behavior at a time. As the student becomes successful, other plans can follow and build upon the existing accomplishments.

2. Find a consequence. Effective consequences can be determined by observing a student carefully and discovering the activities which he really likes to do. Write down these activities which are deemed as possible consequences. From these select the one which could "turn on" the student. It is not always clear why a particular item or activity is a consequence for a child. As someone once said, "students will work for the darnedest things." One twelve-year-old girl liked to collect pictures of soft cuddly animals; therefore her teacher selected this item for her consequence.

It is also difficult to designate a particular consequence to a specific age level. Sometimes a consequence will work as well in changing behavior with a junior high student as it does with a first grader, as the following example will illustrate. A junior high teacher assigned to the English department in a ghetto area school discovered that her homemade cookies were great consequences. One boy expressed, "No one ever made cookies for me before." A first grade teacher also discovered that her homemade cookies were favorite consequences with her young pupils. The children said, "It's like having dessert in school."

As individual students are observed it will become clear that each one has his own hierarchy of consequences. One student may thoroughly enjoy a creative art project and another student could care less. An old adage, "One person's cup of tea is another's poison," applies here. Compiling a list of potential consequences is dependent on keen teacher observations and an understanding of the individual student; therefore, an isolated group of consequences cannot be prescribed for specific age and grade levels.

Most of the time, consequences which are the activities and materials usually found in all classrooms can be used effectively with children. Sometimes, however, the teacher and child may be confronted with what seems to be an insurmountable hurdle. For example, a child who has experienced failure after failure in attempts to work division problems may not try again to receive a check mark "C" or a high percentage grade. In fact, he may not even begin the assigned task. All "natural" consequences fail to reach the student. In these special cases a teach may need to employ extrinsic kinds of consequences, such as food, money, or an early school day dismissal. Teachers are fully cognizant that these consequences are not normally used in a classroom; however, they are willing to try to change the student who is frequently labeled "incorrigible," "immature," or "lazy." They feel it is of utmost importance to reach the impossible child. If the application of extrinsic consequences changes the student's performance, the teacher should continue the plan. It is essential to note that once a certain level of success has been reached, extrinsic consequences are usually no longer necessary. At this point, the fading process should begin. Once the student performs appropriately for a period of time, the extrinsic consequence is gradually changed into more natural consequences such as grades and teacher's praise.

A special classroom exampe will illustrated this fading process. Six young emotionally disturbed children received frequent consequences for a series of small tasks assigned during their first hour of scheduled work activities. If all the tasks were completed in one hour the children also received orange juice and vanilla wafers. Initially the children ate vigorously and talked simultaneously. As the school months elapsed their social graces improved. The children ate smaller portions of the snacks and monitored their own conversations. Meanwhile they had requested and were learning how to serve the cookies and pour the juice. Several months later all the students were participating very appropriately in conversation and generally refusing food. The extrinsic consequence, food, gradually shifted into a very natural consequence, the enjoyment of conversation with friends after a work period.

3. *Discussion and clarification of arrangements.* Before a modification program is implemented, discuss the pending arrangements with the student. The target behavior, its expected change (the goal), and the ensuing consequences should be clarified. "Tom, you seem to have trouble finishing your work even though it is something you can do. Last week you turned in fourteen incompete papers and one complete paper. Let's devise a plan to help you. Each time you complete a paper on time you man have ten minutes of free time to read your library book [his favorite pastime]." The student becomes fully aware of the teacher's expectations. In this example the student must also understand

clearly the time allotted to each assignment, and the teacher must be *consistent* and *immediate* in delivering the consequence. "Good, Tom, you finished your paper on time. You earned ten minutes of free time to read your library book."

For some students, smaller steps of achievement are initially accepted before the final goal is achieved. In Tom's case the teacher might expect him to complete arithmetic papers only. Once he has accomplished this task, then the completion of papers in social studies is expected until he is able to complete papers in all subject areas.

Regular and special teachers often ask, "What do I do with the other students when they see what Elaine gets for doing the same kind of work they are doing?" Two successful techniques have been used by many teachers. (1) The reality of the situation is met. The student with the problem is usually known to the classmates as well as to the teacher; that is, the problem is no secret. After the teacher discusses the arrangements with the troubled student, she can appeal to the other students' value system by requesting their cooperation and encouragement of the student's changing behavior. From time to time the teacher should express her pleasure. "You are a great group. You certainly are helping Elaine change." (2) Some teachers using this approach have intermittently offered a "special something" to the other students. "You are really a fine group to help Elaine. Let's take a ten-minute break and I'll play a new hit song you all like." Or, "Let's take a ten minute break and chat with each other."

4. Plan for evaluation. Is the modification program successful? The level of success is determined by the teacher and based on her experiences with the pupil's past and current performances. The plan is individualized and no predetermined criterion is imposed. If a record is kept of the target behavior occurrences before and during the change, definitive information is available to determine the level of success. One teacher observed that Joe, a social isolate, exchanged conversation with his classmates seven times in twenty-two school days, a total of 110 hours. After a planned program was established to encourage his peer interaction, the student was able to converse with his classmates five times a day. Later this amount increased. The teacher felt that Joe was successful in changing his isolated social behavior.

5. *Fading the modification program (consequence)*. When the changing behavior reaches the desirable goal and stays at that level for a reasonable amount of time, the consequence is faded and eventually eliminated. One example of the fading process has already been discussed. In many modification programs secondary consequences frequently accompany the major consequence. In the case of the student who received free time to read a library book, the teacher's praise, "Good, Tom," accompanied the earned free time. It is often possible to use this secondary consequence in the fading process; that is, Tom's completion of papers was eventually followed by teacher praise only, rather than by the reading of library books.

When Joe was directed to socialize with his peers, he was able to do so; however, as the modification continued, the teacher observed Joe's spontaneous enjoyment of peer interaction. The teacher's application of a consequence faded as the natural consequence of group approval and socialization developed and subsequently maintained Joe's self-directed social conversation.

Another fading process involves a gradual increase of behavior expectations for the same consequence. If, for example, a student was working a half hour for a consequence, the half hour could be extended to an hour and longer as the target behavior changed in the desired direction. The process of fading is *imperative* when synthetic consequences are used initially.

ACCENT ON THE POSITIVE

Behaviors selected for change fall into two major categories—those which need to be increased, e.g., accuracy in seatwork assignments, and those which need to be decreased, e.g., fighting on the playground. The student attracting attention is generally the student exhibiting an inordinate amount of unacceptable behaviors, those which need to be decelerated. There are occasions when a modification plan will focus on the decrease of inappropriate behaviors. HOWEVER, there is another way to change these behaviors. When a student's behavior is unacceptable, the behavior can be restated so that a positive counterpart may be introduced. For example, a student is frequently out of seat, engaging in many distracting actions. The teacher could decelerate his out-of-seat behavior, that is, the child could lose a favorite activity period for being out-of-seat, OR the teacher could say, "You have been out of your seat too often. Sit in your seat and ask permission to leave it. For every twenty minutes that you remain in your seat you will earn two minutes of free time. The extra free time which you earn for remaining in your seat can be added to your recess." The teacher had observed that the student spent 80 percent of his time out-of-seat and 20 percent of his time in-seat. She decided to increase the in-seat behavior, thereby reducing the time spent out-of-seat, rather than vice versa. To help a student acquire appropriate behaviors, restate the inappropriate behavior into a positive counterpart. Apply the consequence to the accepted behavior and Accent the Positive.

It is imperative for the reader to assume that in each cited example, curriculum materials geared to the student's instructional level have been selected. It would be impossible for a student to achieve a prescribed level of performance if the instructional materials were not within his capabilities. The assessment of the student's academic level and the prescription of academic tasks is a complete topic which will not be included here. Once appropriate material has been selected and the student still does not perform, the application of consequences becomes a crucial variable.

The examples which are included in the following pages actually occurred and were successful in regular and special education classrooms. They are offered to you as ideas for consequences, springboards to a modification plan for an individual student. As one college student expressed, "I like the neat things that I see the teachers doing."

Part Two
Develop Positive Performances

ACCELERATE APPROPRIATE BEHAVIOR
Specific Classroom Examples

Goal behavior

Correct spelling of weekly word list.

Consequence

Omission of the final test on Friday.

Arrangement

The teacher wrote each student's spelling words on index cards which were to be used for home study. If the parents felt that their child knew a word, they wrote an "o.k." on the card. Each morning the teacher asked the student to spell the words. Correct words were placed in one stack and the incorrect words were placed in another stack. If the student achieved 100% on the word list on Thursday, she did not have to take the Friday test.

Goal behavior

Accurate completion of academic tasks and demonstrated appropriate social behaviors.

Consequence

Work for wages in school kitchen.

Arrangement

Junior high students received points for academic and social behaviors which had been defined by these students and posted on their classroom bulletin board. The student receiving the highest number of points per day could work in the school kitchen for wages the next day.

Goal behavior

Recognition and pronunciation of phonic lesson words.

Consequence

Typing words on index cards.

Arrangement

If the student recognized and pronounced the words correctly four days in a row, she could use the primary typewriter. Each known word could be typed on an individual card and placed in the student's card file box.

Goal behavior

Learning multiplication tables.

Consequence

Earning pieces of a model car kit.

Arrangement

One piece of a model car was given for each learned multiplication fact. When all the parts had been earned, the junior high student could assemble the car when he had free time.

Goal behavior

Writing numbers 1 to 100 in a sequence on a single worksheet.

Consequence

Teacher's praise and contact.

Arrangement

Praise was given to the child upon successful completion of writing five numbers, until 100 was reached. Later the amount of correctly written numbers had to increase to ten for teacher's praise. As the child's independence in number writing increased, praise decreased; however, the teacher always praised and gave the student a warm arm shake for a completed paper.

Goal behavior

Immediate recognition of rhyming word pairs.

Consequence

Reading the "I know" stack of words to a class-mate.

Arrangement

The student was expected to participate in small group study sessions, self-directed and teacher-directed lessons. A daily test was given. If the rhyming pairs were recognized on the first response, the words were placed in the "I know" stack. At the end of the week the student selected a classmate to listen to her known words.

Goal behavior

Achieving 80 percent or better on reading work-sheets.

Consequence

Graphing progress.

Arrangement

A bar graph was designed and each section was dated. Page number was also indicated. When a reading worksheet was graded, the student colored in the appropriate segments of the section. In a glance the child's accuracy level was seen and signs of progress were visible.

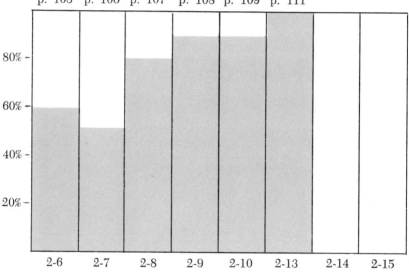

p. 103   p. 106   p. 107   p. 108   p. 109   p. 111

Goal behavior

To learn sight vocabulary and subtraction facts.

Consequence

Earning paper clips which could be exchanged for free time.

Arrangement

A paper clip was given to the student for each learned word or subtraction fact. Each paper clip could be exchanged for one minute of free time. The child never exchangd the clips. He preferred to fasten each earned clip into a chain which was strung on the walls in the classroom. Classmates made favorable comments about the growing chain.

Goal behavior

Finishing mathematics assignments.

Consequence

"Beating the clock."

Arrangement

The student was expected to complete an assignment before the kitchen timer clicked. The student tried to beat the clock. He maintained a record of the number of times he was able to beat the clock.

Goal behavior

Accelerating the number of times a student raised his hand to volunteer an answer during the oral session of math and English lessons.

Consequence

Self-recording.

Arrangement

Each time the student volunteered an answer in math and English he recorded his response by marking a section of graph paper. The graph paper had been labeled as follows:

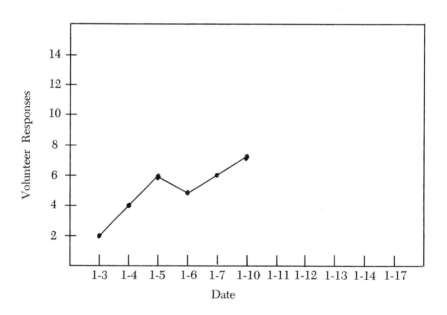

Reliability checks were made by the teacher who recorded the student's volunteer responses at various intervals.

Goal behavior

Learning new reading words.

Consequence

Coloring with a felt pen the one inch sections of a graph measuring 2" × 36".

Arrangement

*New words were presented to the students by the teacher who employed the developmental techniques to teach reading. Following the instruction session the teacher required each student to review the words three times without error. For each word successfully recognized after three trials, the student could color in a box on the **long** graph.*

Goal behavior

Increasing number of correct responses to single digit multiplication problems in a ten-minute period.

Consequence

Token exchange for tutoring session with a third-grade student.

Arrangement

A token was given to the student for every ten correct answers. If five or more tokens were achieved in the ten minute period, the student could help a younger student study arithmetic. (The tutoring sessions had been prearranged with the third grade student's teacher.)

27

Goal behavior

Using the carrying process for the tens and hundreds columns in addition problems.

Consequence

Baseball cards.

Arrangement

Baseball cards were given for each correct answer. Later the student received one card for every three correct answers, then one card for one line of correct answers, and finally a baseball card for one page of correct answers.

Goal behavior

Improving academic performance from the current level of no "turned in" papers.

Consequence

Magic tricks time.

Arrangement

Points were assigned to the ongoing grading system. A=4, B=3, C=2, D=1. Each point represented one minute of free time. If ten or more points were accrued daily, the student could work with the magic trick materials for the number of minutes accrued at the end of the school day.

Goal behavior

Increasing student's work capacity for basic subtraction facts and decreasing their objection and refusal to do subtraction papers.

Consequence

Hot Wheel cars.

Arrangement

Students could advance their Hot Wheel cars one space on the cardboard track for every row of subtraction problems completed correctly within the established time limit. Students reaching the finish line (the first student finished in two months) could keep their earned Hot Wheel cars.

Goal behavior

Finish reading work pages in a fifteen-minute period.

Consequence

Playing with toy animals.

Arrangement

If the student finished the assignments within the specified time he could play with the toy animals for five minutes. Should the work be completed before the work period had elapsed, he could use the remaining time for play.

Goal behavior

Correct completion of an academic task.

Consequence

Field trip.

Arrangement

Immediately upon the correct completion of an assignment, a student was given a ticket. The tickets were exchanged for the Friday afternoon field trip. A pre-determined ticket amount was established so that the students could work toward the goal. The teacher established a 90 percent level of correct performances; hence a student having forty individual assignments a week must receive at least thirty-six tickets for that week.

Goal behavior

Completing phonic worksheets.

Consequence

Watching the ant farm.

Arrangement

If the student completed a phonic worksheet he earned five minutes to watch the ant farm in the classroom.

Goal behavior

Improved spelling accuracy.

Consequence

A plastic figure advanced on the steps of a ladder.

Arrangement

The student was expected to spell four words daily. Two words were new words. The number of new words increased as the student progressed. For each correctly spelled word the student advanced his plastic figure one rung up a pipe cleaner ladder which was suspended from the ceiling.

Goal behavior

Qualitative and quantitative increase in math responses.

Consequence

Playing baseball.

Arrangement

Fifteen sixth grade boys had to achieve a minimum 80 percent accuracy during the one-hour group and individual math session to play in a thirty minute baseball session. During the baseball games the boys kept a continuous record of their batting average which, incidentally, was an enhancement of their math skills.

Goal behavior

Accelerating the accuracy of an independently completed English assignment (usually a fifty minute assignment).

Consequence

Reading a hot rod magazine.

Arrangement

The student earned ten minutes to read a hot rod magazine for every correctly completed English assignment.

Goal behavior

Writing lower case alphabet letters in fifteen minutes without destroying paper.

Consequence

Sticker for every completed, readable letter.

Arrangement

The student received one sticker for each readable letter with a bonus of a decorative seal if a pre-set number of stickers was met. These were kept on daily sticker pages in a special notebook.

Goal behavior

Answering questions to silent reading passages in a fifteen-minute period.

Consequence

Physical education.

Arrangement

Student received an extra five minutes of physical education for each correctly answered question. The earned time was accumulated until the end of each week when the student joined a physical education class. Arrangements between the homeroom teacher and physical education instructor had been made.

Goal behavior

Increasing the number of learned Dolch phrase cards.

Consequence

Free time at game center.

Arrangement

If the student learned three phrase cards beyond the previous day's record within the assigned reading period, he could spend ten minutes at the game center. The teacher had arranged game equipment and materials in a corner of the room.

Goal behavior

Finishing an assignment in thirty minutes.

Consequence

Grooming.

Arrangement

Student and teacher discussed the amount of work which could be completed in a half hour. If the agreed upon assignment was finished, the girl earned free time to brush and comb her hair. Incidental learning developed from this consequence. The girl's total personal appearance gradually improved as she became interested in hair styles, selection of clothing, and skin care. When her work habits began to approximate the level of her peers, the teacher was able to set aside some time each week to discuss fashions with all the girls in the classroom.

Goal behavior

Raising hand for teacher attention.

Consequence

Pop bottle caps.

Arrangement

One bottle cap was given each time the student raised his hand at appropriate intervals. During the initial days of this arrangement the teacher said, "Good, George, you raised your hand," and then she presented the bottle cap.

Goal behavior

Placing rubber numerals one to ten in a correct left to right order.

Consequence

Chalkboard drawing.

Arrangement

If the student could place the numerals in a sequential left to right order within a five-minute period, she could draw at the chalkboard for five minutes.

Goal behavior

Completion and 90 percent accuracy on individual worksheets.

Consequence

Weekly display of good papers on hall bulletin board.

Arrangement

Student saved all his papers completed on time with 90 percent accuracy and placed them in a designated folder. On Friday, he displayed them as a "Big Splash" on the hall bulletin board.

Goal behavior

Increased productivity and correct responses in reading workbook.

Consequence

Play a game on the bowling machine.

Arrangement

For each workbook page completed with 100 percent accuracy, the student played two games on the bowling machine. For each workbook page completed with 80-99 percent accuracy, the student played one game.

Goal behavior

Auditory recognition of consonant sounds.

Consequence

Making a paper dachshund cut-out "grow."

Arrangement

When the student learned a new consonant sound, a mid-section piece was added to a paper dachshund, displayed on the bulletin board.

Goal behavior

To complete work in a given period of time.

Consequence

Engage in activities in a free time room.

Arrangement

If a student completed specific assignments he could go into a converted small storage room and engage in free time activities. "Junk" type items including a broken phonograph, old wall switch plates, scraps of lumber, pieces of tile, etc. were available. A kitchen timer was set for a specific time, thereby reminding the student when the free period was over.

Goal behavior

Completion of work in blocks of time and achievement of 80 percent or better accuracy.

Consequence

Games.

Arrangement

Assignments according to subject matter were made in blocks of time so that an opportunity for free time could be earned after each academic block. The student was free to play with educational type games in the classroom. Commercial and many teacher-made games were changed frequently to keep the children's interest. Game time was a ten-minute session.

Goal behavior

Completing work assigned within a given period, 9:00-10:30 A.M.

Consequence

Juice and cookies.

Arrangement

The students who completed the work assigned to the first half of their morning activities could participate in a juice and cookie break.

Goal behavior

Increased accuracy on academic worksheets.

Consequence

Pupil placed paper for display on bulletin board.

Arrangement

If the student had no more than one error on a paper he could place it on the room's main bulletin board.

Goal behavior

Completion of academic tasks.

Consequence

Using an adding machine. (Language Master or Systems 80 can also be used.)

Arrangement

If the student completed his academic tasks assigned to a time block, e.g. 9:00-10:30 A.M., he earned fifteen minutes to use the adding machine. His enthusiasm to calculate on the machine enhanced the incidental learning of addition facts.

Goal behavior

Immediate recognition of two-digit numbers, 50-99.

Consequence

Progression through the cards of a paper train and achievement of goal—train engineer.

Arrangement

Two-digit numbers were written on single sheets of paper which were clipped to cars of the paper train. The student moved from the caboose to other cars by the correct identification of numbers. If the student missed a number he returned to the caboose and began the progression again. Each time the student reached the cab of the train a tally mark was placed on the cab.

Goal behavior

Recognition of sight-word reading vocabulary.

Consequence

Beads for a necklace.

Arrangement

For each learned word the child received a bead; however, if a word was missed during the review sessions a bead was returned. When a pre-selected number of beads had been accumulated, the student was given time to string the beads.

Goal behavior

To increase a shy child's minimal talking to teacher and peers.

Consequence

Construction paper slips with decorative sticker seals.

Arrangement

When the student talked or responded to teacher-pupil conversation, she received a decorative seal mounted on the construction paper. These slips of paper could be carried home if the pupil elected to do this.

Goal behavior

The recognition of difficult reading words.

Consequence

Shoot at difficult words on a target with a suction cup gun.

Arrangement

The student studied the difficult words during assigned sessions and during free time. He was given a test at the end of the day. If he knew the words he was then able to shoot the difficult words written on the target board, an old converted chalk board.

ADDITIONAL CONSEQUENCE ACTIVITIES

Consequences

1. Write and stage TV commercials.

2. Prepare a puppet show.

3. Work at listening station or area where phonograph with headset equipment is available. Teacher-made tapes and commercial recordings were available at stations.

4. Develop transparencies for overhead projector.

5. Puzzles, dot-to-dot pictures, and brain teasers.

6. Hard work certificate.

7. Assemble 250-piece puzzle. Completed puzzle is mounted on heavy cardboard and sprayed with plastic coating.

8. Write riddles.

9. Blueprint paper, graph paper, and pencils for floor plan drawing.

10. Sewing equipment for home economics students.

11. Totem pole construction.

12. Mural painting.

13. Play popular records.

14. Work with scrap materials.

15. Movie projector operator for school building.

16. Teacher's assistant to run ditto machine.

17. Workshop time.

18. Informal cooking area.

19. Work with art materials and junk.

20. Look at mail order catalogues.

21. Guide visitors on a tour of the school building.

22. Leave school one-half hour early.

23. Talking time with peers.

24. Listening to an older student tell a story.

25. Teacher's smile.

26. Stars, decorative seals, or ink-stamp pictures on papers.

27. Ride the school elevator.

28. Daily grade cards.

29. Compliment the child in front of others.

30. Work on crossword puzzles using plastic overlays.

Part Three
Decrease Negative Performances

RESTATE THE BEHAVIOR
Specific Classroom Examples

Exhibited behavior

Students had been five to ten minutes late in arriving for class.

Goal behavior

Arriving on time or a few minutes before class.

Consequence

Hearing a mystery story.

Arrangement

Teacher read a short segment of an exciting mystery story for the first few minutes after lunch one day, after which she announced that it would be continued during the first ten minutes of class each morning. Those present would have a chance to hear what happened next.

Exhibited behavior

Talking to the teacher without permission.

Goal behavior

Raising hand and being recognized before speaking.

Consequence

Using microscope.

Arrangement

The student was given five metal washers when he entered the classroom. Each time he talked without permission he "paid" the teacher one washer. At the end of the day, each washer remainng in his possession was worth an allotted period of time to be spent working with the microscope.

Exhibited behavior

Facial grimaces.

Goal behavior

To develop appropriate facial expressions.

Consequence

Peer approval.

Arrangement

Three children seated in close proximity to the student expressed at intervals, "Good, Paul, you are not making faces." When the student's facial expressions were pleasant, any one of the three students said, "Great, Paul, you are smiling."

Exhibited behavior

Messy papers, torn corners, sloppy erasures, and doodling in margins.

Goal behavior

Neatly done work.

Consequence

"Paper of the day."

Arrangement

The teacher watched or helped the child until one neatly done paper was turned in. The child was praised for his neat work and his paper was displayed prominently outside the classroom as "paper of the day."

Exhibited behavior

Student requires inordinate amount of teacher attention.

Goal behavior

Longer periods of times when the student can work independently.

Consequence

Teacher attention.

Arrangement

For each fifteen-minute (or at first, five or ten minute) period that the child worked independently he received a token. At the end of a two-hour period (or less, depending on the child) each token was worth two minutes of direct, uninterrupted teacher attention.

Exhibited behavior

Spending long periods of time in the hall while going to and from the restroom.

Goal behavior

Prompt return to classroom.

Consequence

Use of a stopwatch and self-recording.

Arrangement

The operation of a stopwatch was explained to the student. He was given the watch when he left the room and was required to time the minutes which he spent outside the classroom. He recorded this time on a sheet of paper as a visible reminder of his efforts to decrease hallway time.

Exhibited behavior

Pencil chewing.

Goal behavior

To refrain from chewing pencils.

Consequence

Work on model airplane.

Arrangement

Twelve tokens were placed on the teacher's desk at the beginning of each hour. The student was given one token for every five minutes he maintained the desired behavior. The student placed the earned tokens in a bank (a small cardboard box). As the student improved, the five-minute period was gradually lengthened to longer segments of time for tokens. One token was removed each time the student chewed on his pencil. Ten tokens were exchanged for a ten-minute block of time to work on model airplane.

Exhibited behavior

Crying, as attention-getting behavior.

Goal behavior

To complete a school day without crying.

Consequence

"Medals" for bravery.

Arrangement

Medals were constructed of brightly colored paper and odd scraps (gummed notebook hole ring, stickers, braid, rickrack, etc.). At first one was given and pinned on for each assignment the child completed without crying; this was later reduced and a large medal was given at the end of each day in which no crying occurred. Praise or comments for medals were given by older classmates and adult personnel.

Exhibited behavior

Throwing food in cafeteria.

Goal behavior

To eat the noon meal without throwing food.

Consequence

Twenty extra minutes to stay up before bedtime.

Arrangement

Parents and teacher had agreed to the plan before the student was informed. For each noon period the student received a 3 × 5 card labeled:

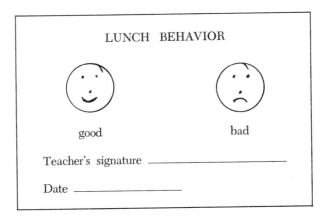

He took the card home and if a smiling face was checked he was permitted to stay up an extra twenty minutes before bedtime. Later the parents included the breakfast and supper meals in this arrangement.

Exhibited behavior

Student balked at doing corrections on his math errors after his work had been checked and the errors explained.

Goal behavior

Student correcting mistakes satisfactorily.

Consequence

Drawing a slip from the "surprise box."

Arrangement

In the classroom there was a cardboard box covered with crepe paper. When a student had finished his work and completed the correction of his mistakes satisfactorily (according to pre-set teacher criteria) he had earned the right to draw a slip from the box. On the slips were many things, limited only by the teacher's imagination: i.e., "You may now do a dot-to-dot picture," a joke, a cartoon clipped from a child's magazine, "Draw a picture of the funniest house you can imagine," "Go get a drink of water," "Feed the gerbils," a code with a message to decipher etc., always with an element of "**surprise**." If the student did not do his corrections he could not draw a slip.

Exhibited behavior

The student spent too much time daydreaming before starting an assignment.

Goal behavior

Getting right to work.

Consequence

Raised "flag."

Arrangement

As soon as the student began to work on the assignment, the teacher raised a flag on his desk. The raised flag also served as a reminder to continue working. The flag was a wooden paint stick mixer with the tip end painted red. It was mounted on the edge of the desk and could be raised or lowered when necessary.

Exhibited behavior

Undesirable playground behavior, e.g., hitting others, twisting swings, bumping a child on the next swing.

Goal behavior

To develop appropriate playground activities.

Consequence

Play record player.

Arrangement

The number of occurrences of these undesirable behaviors during a twenty-minute recess period were counted. If the number decreased from the previous day's record, the child received a chip which could be traded in for time to play the record player.

Exhibited behavior

Sucking or chewing on fingers during play period.

Goal behavior

To play without placing fingers in mouth.

Consequence

Candy.

Arrangement

The child received a piece of candy for each recess period when he did not place fingers in his mouth.

Exhibited behavior

Excessive pencil sharpening.

Goal behavior

Sharpening pencil only when necessary.

Consequence

Pencils.

Arrangement

This student was very fond of pencils. He was given one pencil at the end of the morning if he had not sharpened his other pencils unnecessarily, and given another at the end of the day if he had refrained from excessive pencil sharpening in the afternoon. This was eventually decreased to one pencil a day and later to one pencil a week.

54

Exhibited behavior

The student rested his head on the desk an excessive number of times during a work period.

Goal behavior

To complete assignments without resting head on desk.

Consequence

Teacher's praise and a star.

Arrangement

At various intervals the teacher said, "Good Boy" when the student's head was not resting on his desk. The student received a star for each paper completed with no head rests.

Exhibited behavior

Excessive tardiness.

Goal behavior

Acquisition of "on time for class" behavior.

Consequence

A daily chart of "on time for classes" was signed by parents.

Arrangement

A daily chart, indicating the starting time of the student's departmental class sessions, was made by the homeroom teacher. The student carried the daily chart to each class where the teacher indicated "ontime" or "not on time." The daily chart was carried home, signed by the parents, and retured to school where the student kept a log of the charts.

Exhibited behavior

Excessive out-of-seat movement during study period.

Goal behavior

Remaining in seat during study period.

Consequence

Free time to talk to peers.

Arrangement

When the student reduced his out-of-seat behavior he received free time to chat with a peer outside the classroom. The following system was established. If the student remained in his seat all the time, he received ten minutes of free time. If he left his seat one time he earned only five minutes of free time. If he left his seat two times he earned only one minute of free time. The latter occurred only once because the student realized one minute was not long enough for "chatting."

Exhibited behavior

Student's excessive talking without permission to classmate(s) during work periods.

Goal behavior

Silence during work sessions.

Consequence

Time to work on desired project.

Arrangement

For each fifty-minute period of the school day in which the student did not talk without permission, he received ten minutes of free time. Since there were five fifty-minute periods, it was possible for the student to accumulate fifty minutes of free time. The earned time was spent on a "pet" project during sixth hour, the homeroom period.

Exhibited behavior

Unnecessary laughing during the first hour of academic work.

Goal behavior

Concentrating on work.

Consequence

Time to laugh.

Arrangement

Student received two minutes of free time to laugh for every twenty minutes of not laughing but concentrating on work activities.

Exhibited behavior

Excessive chin scratching during typing and bookkeeping sessions.

Goal behavior

Refraining from chin scratching.

Consequence

Playing pool.

Arrangement

The student received a token for every five minutes he refrained from chin scratching. Each token was exchange for one minute of pool-playing during the noon hour.

Exhibited behavior

Excessive movement of legs for knee-knocking.

Goal behavior

No movement of legs in above fashion.

Consequence

Listening to teacher's praise via "walkie talkies."

Arrangement

During seatwork activities the teacher relayed "Good boy" on the walkie talkie for every two minutes the boy refrained from knee-knocking.

Exhibited behavior

Leaving desk and wandering around the classroom.

Goal behavior

Remaining seated during a thirty-minute work period.

Consequence

Gumdrops.

Arrangement

If the student remained seated for a thirty-minute interval he received a gumdrop. Later the time was extended to an hour per gumdrop. Occasionally the teacher gave gumdrops to the entire class.

Exhibited behavior

Child's negative verbalizations such as: "I don't know anything," "I'm no good."

Goal behavior

Positive expressions of self-worth.

Consequence

Correct marks and positive comments (verbal or written).

Arrangement

For each correct written response, e.g., answer to a math problem or to a social studies question, a correct mark "C" was indicated with a felt pen. Written comments, such as "You are improving," "Great," and "Keep up the good work," were also written on the student's paper.

Exhibited behavior

Vying for peer and teacher attention.

Goal behavior

Directing attention to school tasks.

Consequence

Free time and work with puppets in couselor's office.

Arrangement

If talkouts were below a pre-selected number during the 10:00-10:45 period, the student could have ten minutes of free activity in the counselor's office. That is if the weekly talkout average fell below the previous week's count, the student could go to the counselor's office to develop a puppet show. This arragement had been written into a contract signed by the student, teacher, and counselor. The boy later decided he wanted more free time so he requested that his talkouts be counted during another forty-five-minute work session so he could earn fifteen minutes of free time.

Exhibited behavior

Too many "F" and "D" grades.

Goal behavior

Developing an academic performance which was eligible for "A," "B," or "C" letter grades.

Consequence

A prize.

Arrangement

A prize with a stated point value was selected by the student who earned points for academic work, scaled to grades A=6, B=4, C=2. The student recorded his daily progress until the points reached the pre-selected prize value.

ADDITIONAL CONSEQUENCE ACTIVITIES

Consequences

1. Play with clay.

2. Grade papers.

3. Straighten shelves.

4. Care for class pets.

5. Leader of activities.

6. Deliver messages to other classroom.

7. Choice of seat on school bus.

8. Smiling Sams ☺ on papers.

9. Correct marks by *all* correct responses.

10. Answer the school telephone.

11. Work with microscope and an array of mounted slides.

12. Devise code with teacher or another child and send messages.

13. Polaroid picture of the "student of the day" or week is displayed on bulletin board in main lobby.

14. Student uses tape recorder to prepare original tapes.

15. "Buying off" assignments with accumulated tokens.

16. Choose story to be read by teacher or librarian.

17. Use a stopwatch or kitchen timer to time work.

18. Self-graphing of academic or social progress.

19. Conduct a science experiment with teacher or classmate.

20. Immediate correction of work.

21. Earn a movie (in classroom) and treat by saving points distributed on a systematic basis.

22. Work agreement between student and teacher.

23. Chocolate milk for lunch or snack.

24. Room host: assist visitors to classroom; introduce guests to peers; explain routine.

25. Watch educational TV.

26. A visit from a favorite staff members, i.e., counselor, nurse, principal, volunteer.

27. Time to talk to teacher.

28. Comb, barrettes, mirror, ribbons for special grooming time.

29. Free time.

30. Teacher's praise.